FINGERPICKING
Christmas

ISBN 978-0-634-06247-6

Visit Hal Leonard Online at www.halleonard.com

HAL•LEONARD®
CORPORATION
7777 W. BLUEMOUND RD. P.O. BOX 13819 MILWAUKEE, WI 53213

INTRODUCTION TO FINGERSTYLE GUITAR

Fingerstyle (a.k.a. fingerpicking) is a guitar technique that means you literally pick the strings with your right-hand fingers and thumb. This contrasts with the conventional technique of strumming and playing single notes with a pick (a.k.a. flatpicking). For fingerpicking, you can use any type of guitar: acoustic steel-string, nylon-string classical, or electric.

THE RIGHT HAND
The most common right-hand position is shown here.

Use a high wrist; arch your palm as if you were holding a ping-pong ball. Keep the thumb outside and away from the fingers, and let the fingers do the work rather than lifting your whole hand.

The thumb generally plucks the bottom strings with downstrokes on the left side of the thumb and thumbnail. The other fingers pluck the higher strings using upstrokes with the fleshy tip of the fingers and fingernails. The thumb and fingers should pluck one string per stroke and not brush over several strings.

Another picking option you may choose to use is called hybrid picking (a.k.a. plectrum-style fingerpicking). Here, the pick is usually held between the thumb and first finger, and the three remaining fingers are assigned to pluck the higher strings.

THE LEFT HAND
The left-hand fingers are numbered 1 through 4.

Be sure to keep your fingers arched, with each joint bent; if they flatten out across the strings, they will deaden the sound when you fingerpick. As a general rule, let the strings ring as long as possible when playing fingerstyle.

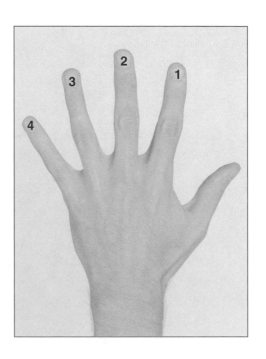

Angels We Have Heard on High

Traditional French Carol
Translated by James Chadwick

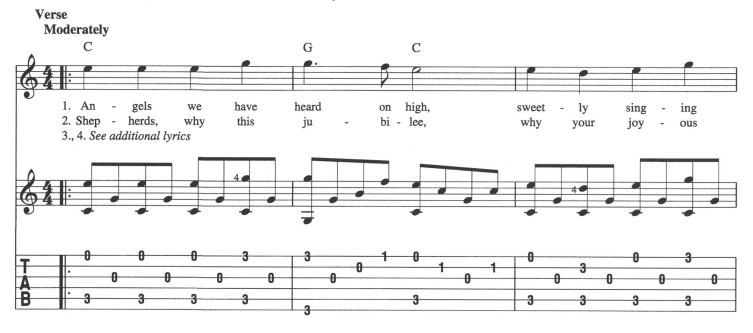

1. An - gels we have heard on high, sweet - ly sing - ing
2. Shep - herds, why this ju - bi - lee, why your joy - ous
3., 4. *See additional lyrics*

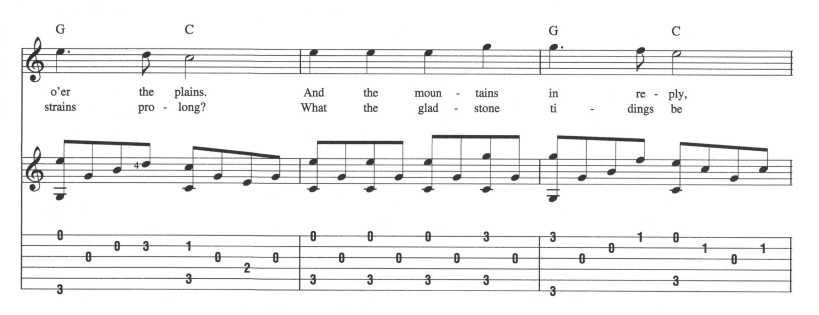

o'er the plains. And the moun - tains in re - ply,
strains pro - long? What the glad - stone ti - dings be

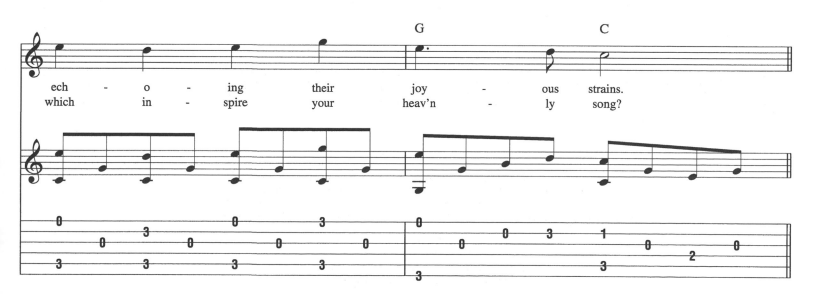

ech - o - ing their joy - ous strains.
which in - spire your heav'n - ly song?

Chorus

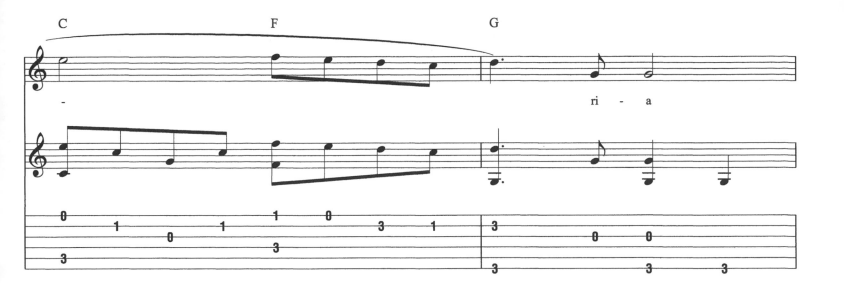

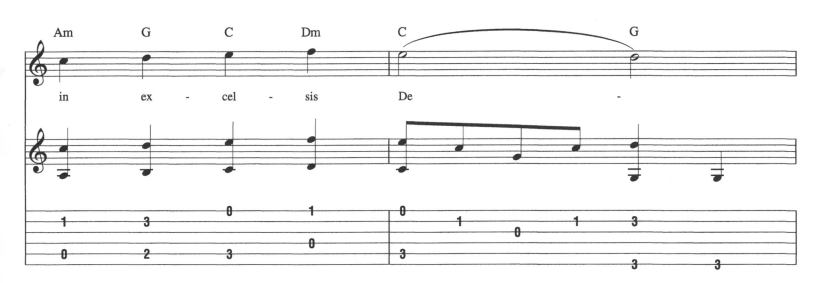

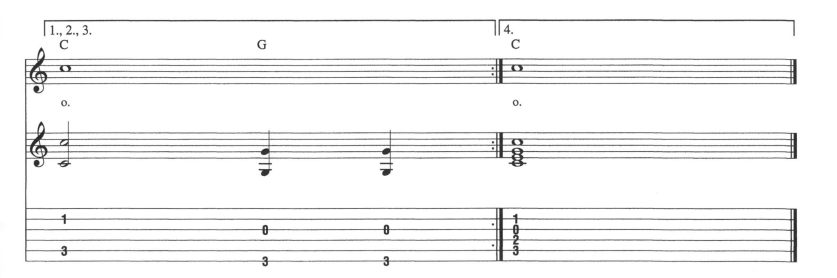

Additional Lyrics

3. Come to Bethlehem and see
   Him whose birth the angels sing;
   Come adore on bended knee
   Christ the Lord, the newborn King.

4. See within a manger laid
   Jesus, Lord of heaven and earth!
   Mary, Joseph, lend your aid,
   With us sing our Savior's birth.

Away in a Manger

Traditional
Words by John T. McFarland (v.3)
Music by James R. Murray

I Saw Three Ships

Traditional English Carol

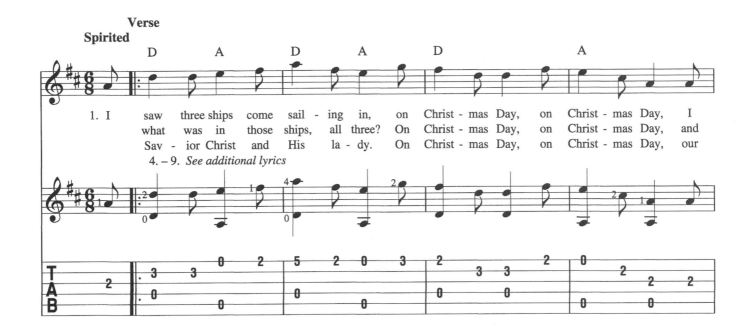

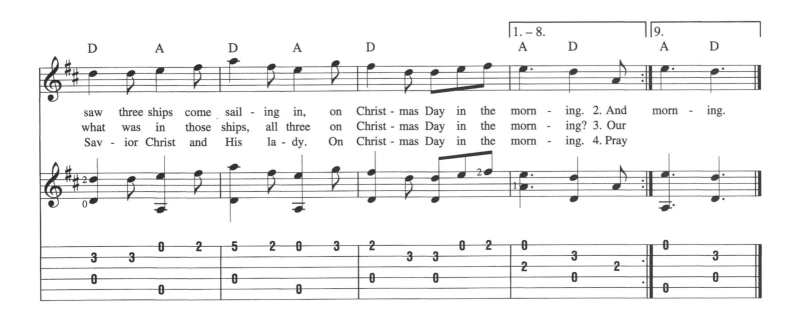

Additional Lyrics

4. Pray, whither sailed those ships all three?
5. O, they sailed into Bethlehem.
6. And all the bells on earth shall ring,
7. And all the angels in heaven sing,
8. And all the souls on earth shall sing,
9. Then let us all rejoice again!

Deck the Hall

Traditional Welsh Carol

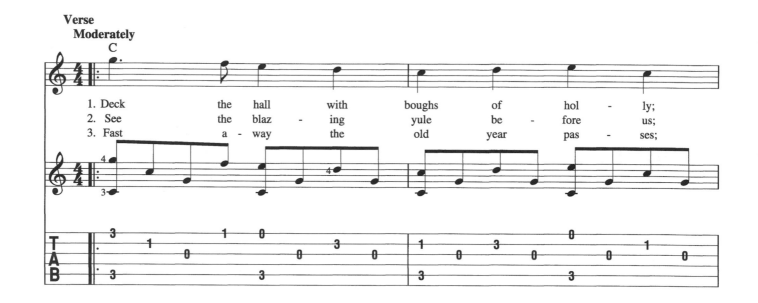

1. Deck the hall with boughs of hol - ly;
2. See the blaz - ing yule be - fore us;
3. Fast a - way the old year pas - ses;

fa, la, la, la, la, la, la, la, la. 'Tis the sea - son
fa, la, la, la, la, la, la, la, la. Strike the harp and
fa, la, la, la, la, la, la, la, la. Hail the new, ye

to be jol - ly; fa, la, la, la, la, la, la, la, la.
join the chor - us; fa, la, la, la, la, la, la, la, la.
lads and las - ses; fa, la, la, la, la, la, la, la, la.

Don we now our gay ap-par-el; fa, la, la, la, la, la,
Fol - low me in mer - ry mea - sure; fa, la, la, la, la, la,
Sing we joy - ous, all to-geth - er; fa, la, la, la, la, la,

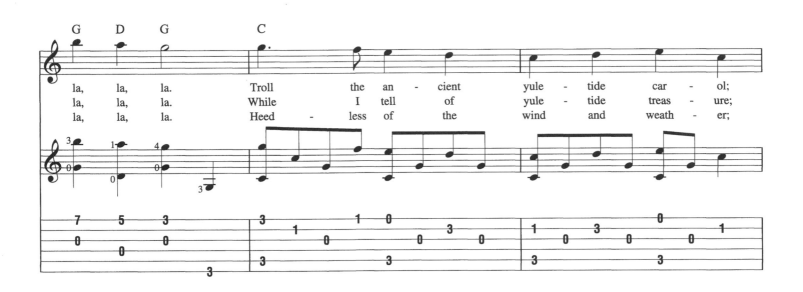

la, la, la. Troll the an - cient yule - tide car - ol;
la, la, la. While I tell of yule - tide treas - ure;
la, la, la. Heed - less of the wind and weath - er;

fa, la, la, la, la, la, la, la, la. la, la, la.
fa, la, la, la, la, la, la, la, la.
fa, la, la, la, la, la,

The First Noël

17th Century English Carol
Music from W. Sandys' Christmas Carols

Verse
Moderately slow

1. The first Noël, the an- gels did say, was to
look- ed up and saw a star, was shin-ing
by the light of that same star, three
4., 5., 6. See additional lyrics

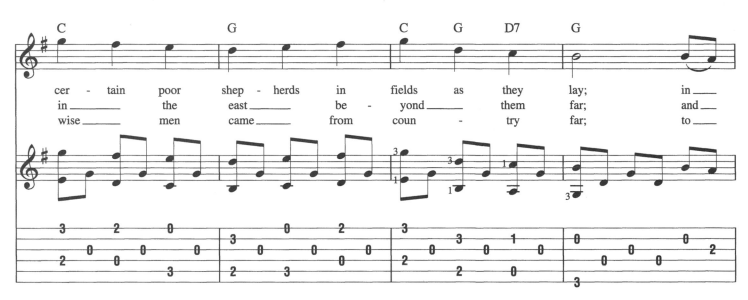

cer- tain poor shep- herds in fields as they lay; in
in the east be- yond them far; and
wise men came from coun- try far; to

fields where they lay keep- ing their sheep, on a
to the earth it gave great light, and
seek for a king was their in- tent, and to

Additional Lyrics

4. This star drew nigh to the northwest,
O'er Bethlehem it took its rest;
And there it did both stop and stay,
Right over the place where Jesus lay.

5. Then entered in those wise men three,
Full reverently upon the knee;
And offered there His presence,
Their gold, and myrrh, and frankincense.

6. Then let us all with one accord
Sing praises to our heav'nly Lord;
That hath made heav'n and earth of naught,
And with His blood mankind hath bought.

Go, Tell It on the Mountain

African-American Spiritual
Verses by John W. Work, Jr.

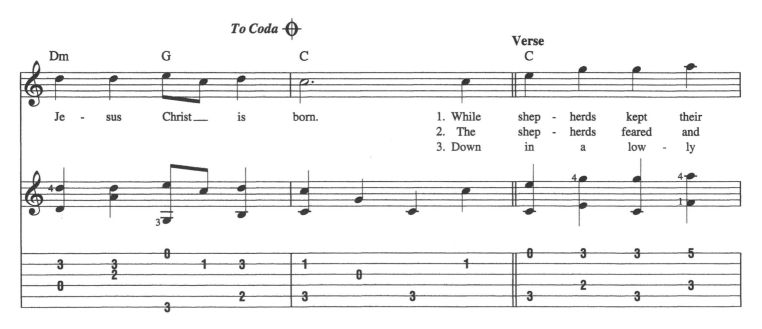

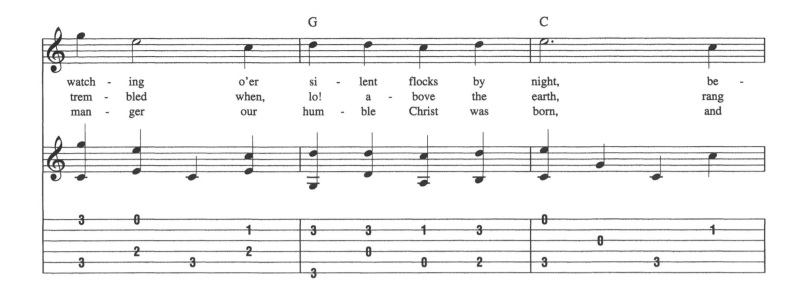

watch - ing o'er si - lent flocks by night, be -
trem - bled when, lo! a - bove the earth, rang
man - ger our hum - ble Christ was born, and

hold, through - out the heav - ens there shone a ho - ly
out the an - gel cho - rus that hailed our Sav - ior's
God sent us sal - va - tion that bless - ed Christ - mas

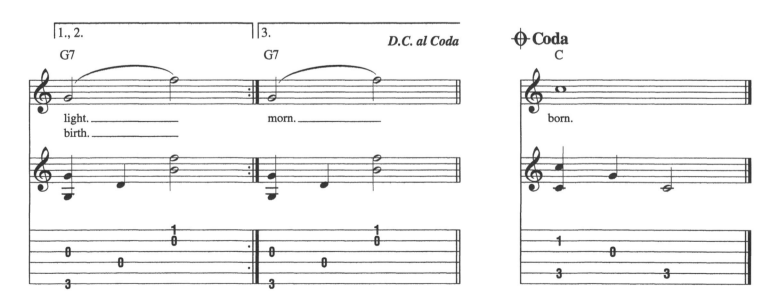

D.C. al Coda   ⊕ **Coda**

1., 2.   3.

light. _____   morn. _____   born.
birth. _____

God Rest Ye Merry, Gentlmen

19th Century English Carol

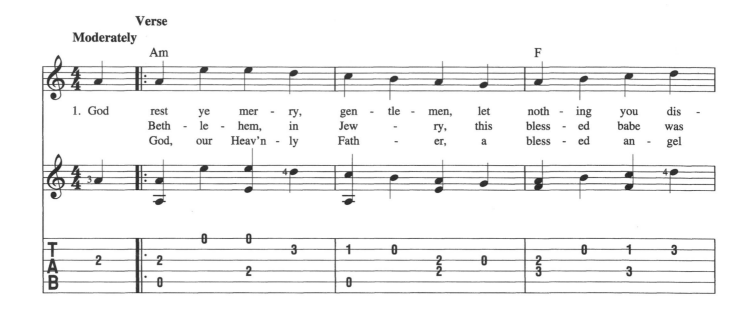

Verse
Moderately

1. God rest ye mer - ry, gen - tle - men, let noth - ing you dis -
Beth - le - hem, in Jew - ry, this bless - ed babe was
God, our Heav'n - ly Fath - er, a bless - ed an - gel

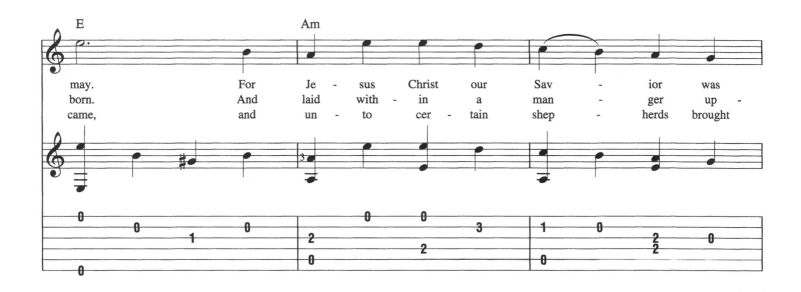

may. For Je - sus Christ our Sav - ior was
born. And laid with - in a man - ger up -
came, and un - to cer - tain shep - herds brought

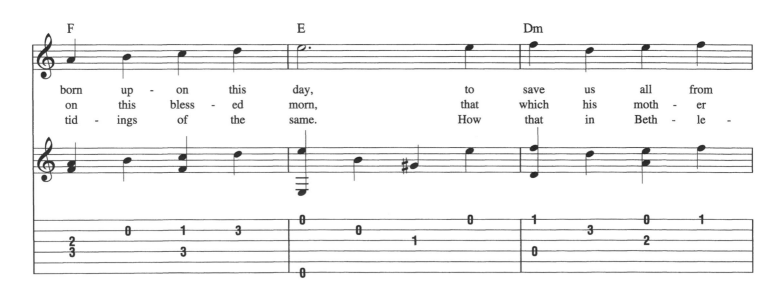

born up - on this day, to save us all from
on this bless - ed morn, that which his moth - er
tid - ings of the same. How that in Beth - le -

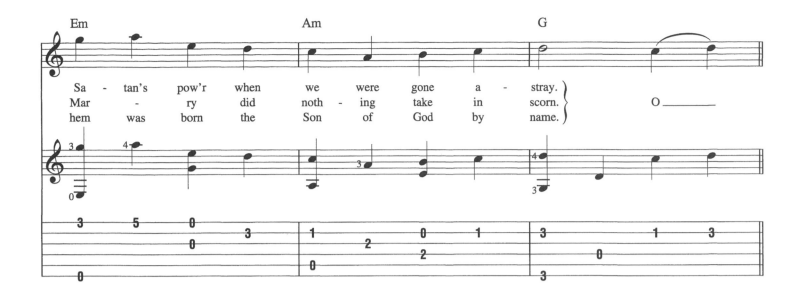

Sa - tan's pow'r when we were gone a - stray. ⎫
Mar - ry did the noth - ing take in scorn. ⎬ O _____
hem was born the Son of God by name. ⎭

Chorus

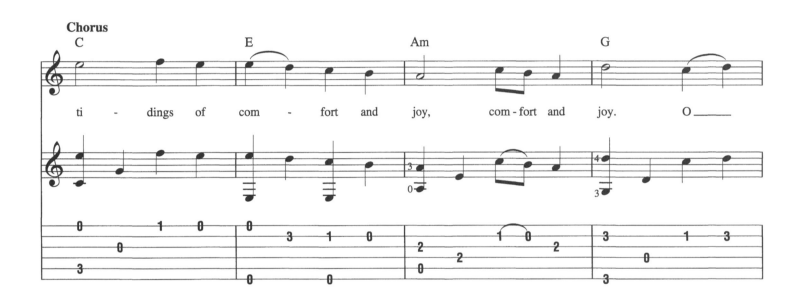

ti - dings of com - fort and joy, com - fort and joy. O _____

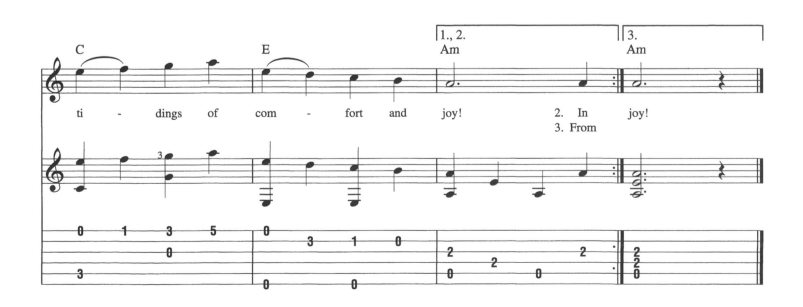

ti - dings of com - fort and joy! 2. In joy!
3. From

Good King Wenceslas

Words by John M. Neale
Music from Piae Cantiones

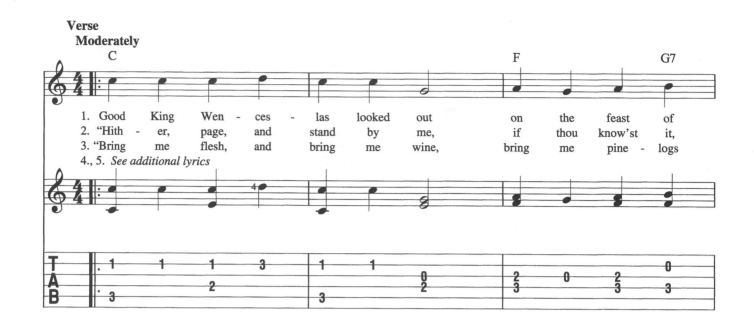

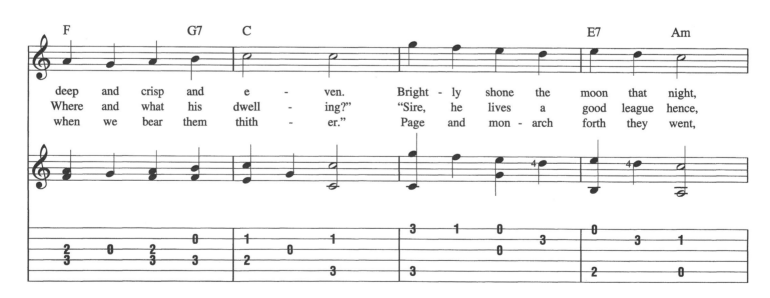

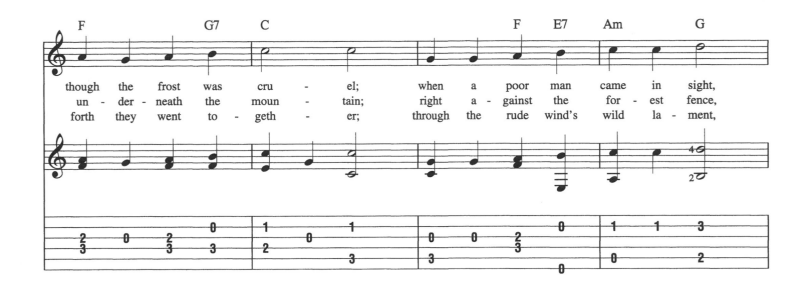

though the frost was cru - el; when a poor man came in sight,
un - der - neath the moun - tain; right a - gainst the for - est fence,
forth they went to - geth - er; through the rude wind's wild la - ment,

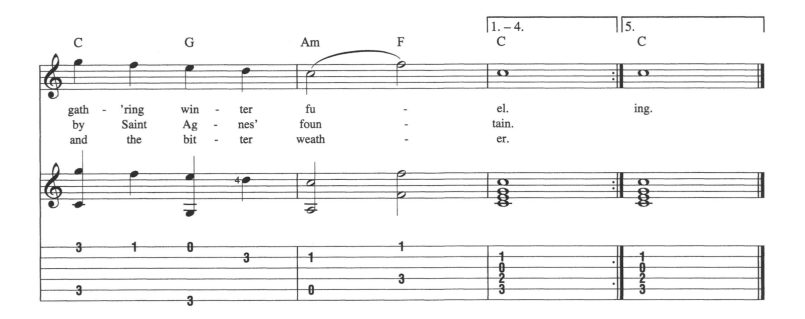

gath - 'ring win - ter fu - el.
by Saint Ag - nes' foun - tain.
and the bit - ter weath - er.

ing.

Additional Lyrics

4. "Sire, the night is darker now,
   And the wind blows stronger;
   Fails my heart, I know not how,
   I can go not longer."
   "Mark my footsteps, my good page,
   Tread thou in them boldly:
   Thou shalt find the winter's rage
   Freeze thy blood less coldly."

5. In his master's steps he trod,
   Where the snow lay dinted;
   Heat was in the very sod
   Which the saint has printed.
   Therefore, Christian men, be sure,
   Wealth or rank possessing;
   Ye who now will bless the poor,
   Shall yourselves find blessing.

Hark! The Herald Angels Sing

Words by Charles Wesley
Altered by George Whitefield
Music by Felix Mendelssohn-Bartholdy
Arranged by William H. Cummings

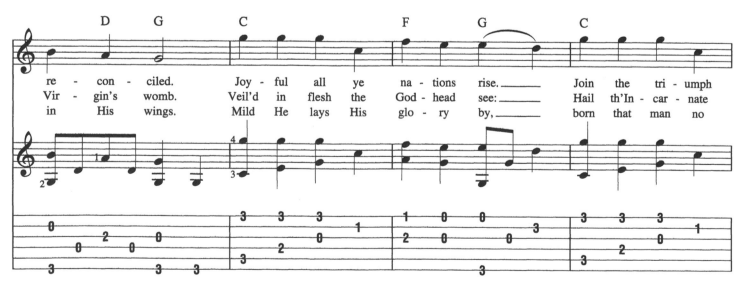

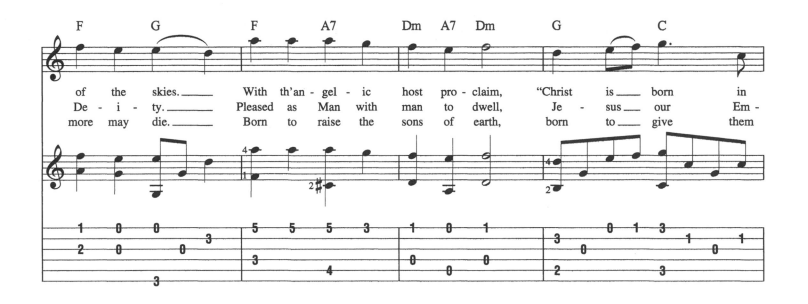

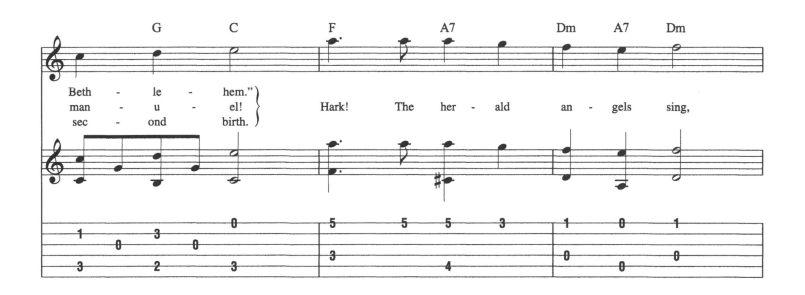

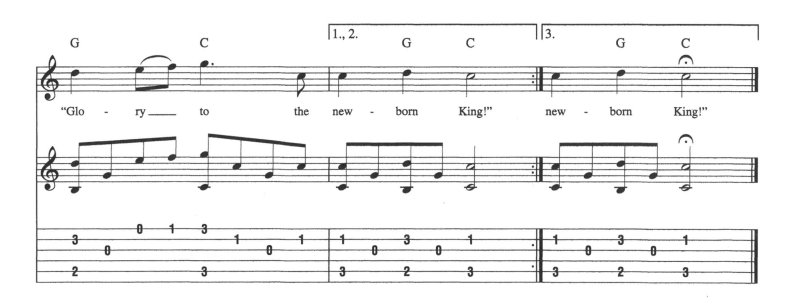

It Came Upon the Midnight Clear

Words by Edmund H. Sears
Traditional English Melody
Adapted by Arthur Sullivan

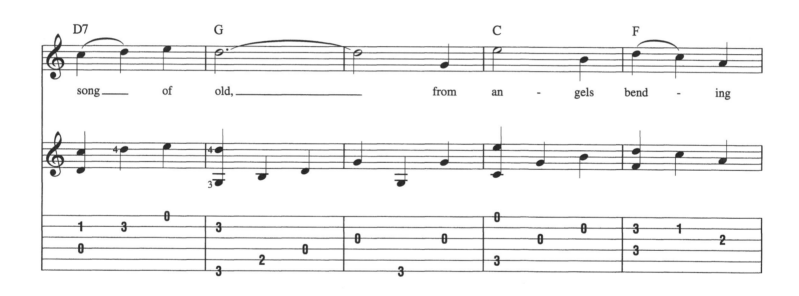

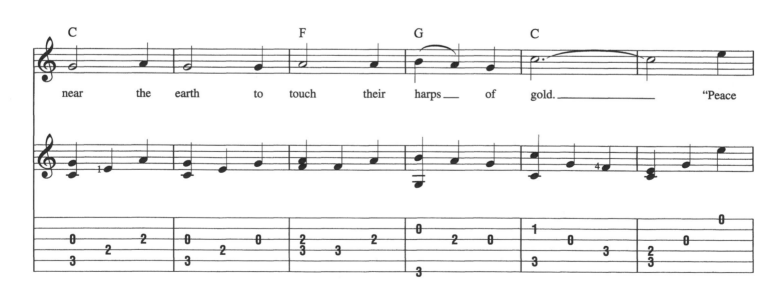

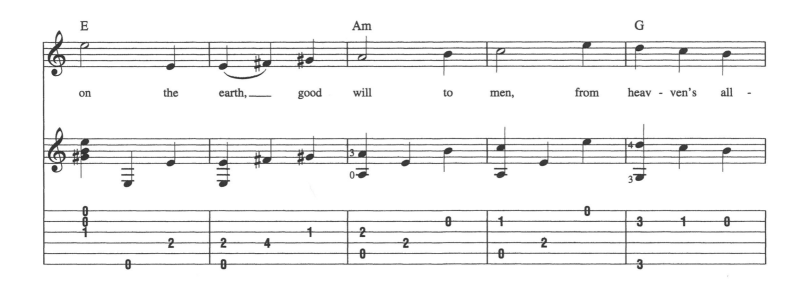

on the earth, ___ good will to men, from heav - ven's all -

gra - cious King." _____ The world in sol - emn

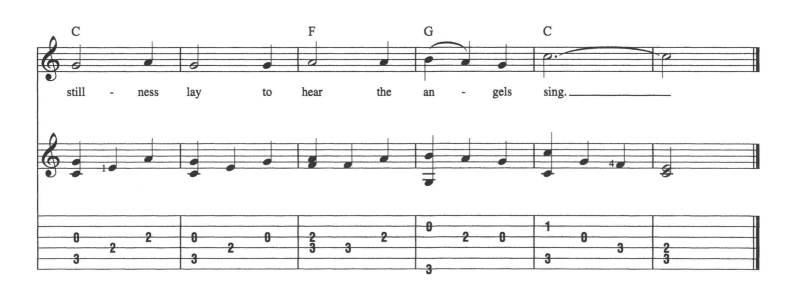

still - ness lay to hear the an - gels sing. _____

Jingle Bells

Words and Music by J. Pierpont

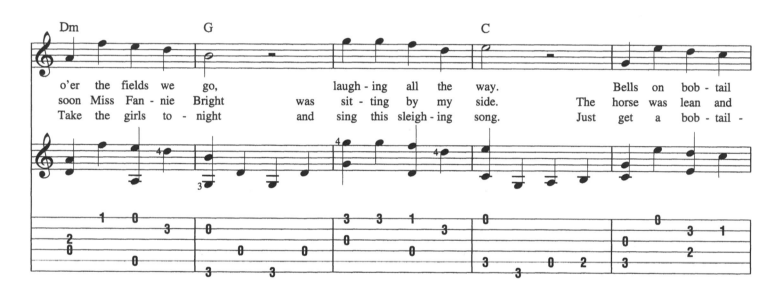

Joy to the World

Words by Isaac Watts
Music by George Frideric Handel

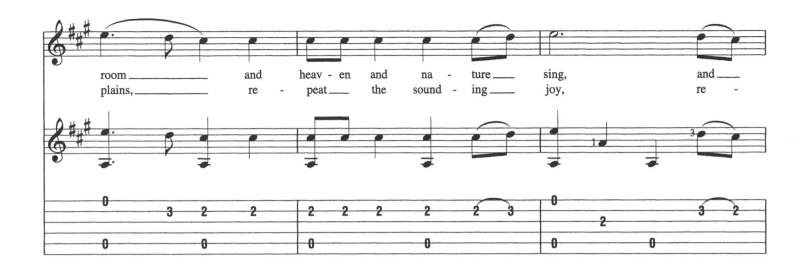

Additional Lyrics

3. No more let sin, and sorrow grow,
   Nor thorns infest the ground;
   He comes to make His blessings flow
   Far as the curse is found,
   Far as the curse is found,
   Far as, far as the curse is found.

4. He rules the world with truth and grace,
   And makes the nations prove
   The glories of His righteousness,
   And wonders of His love,
   And wonders of His love,
   And wonders, wonders of His love.

O Christmas Tree

Traditional German Carol

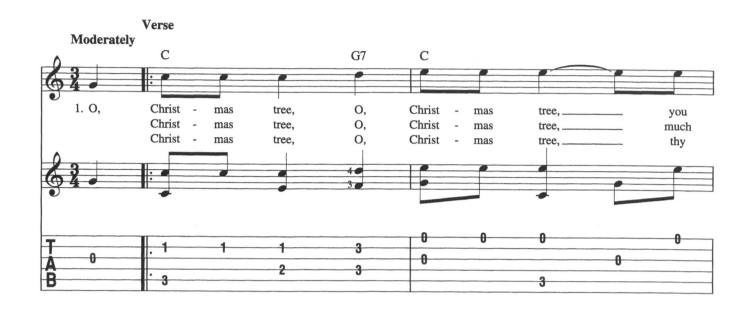

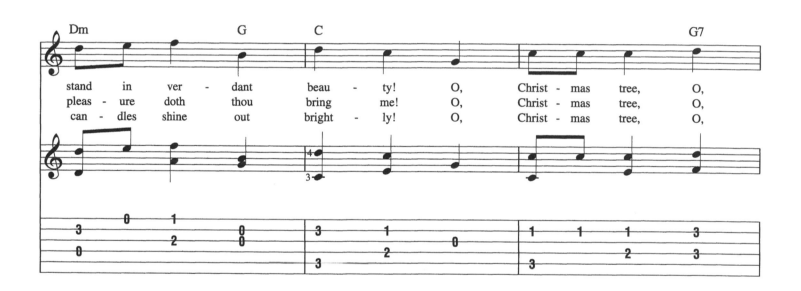

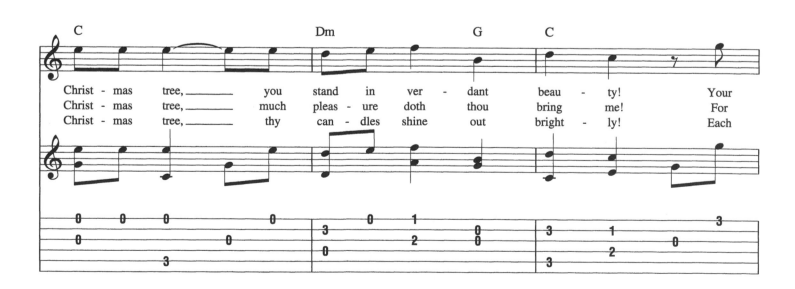

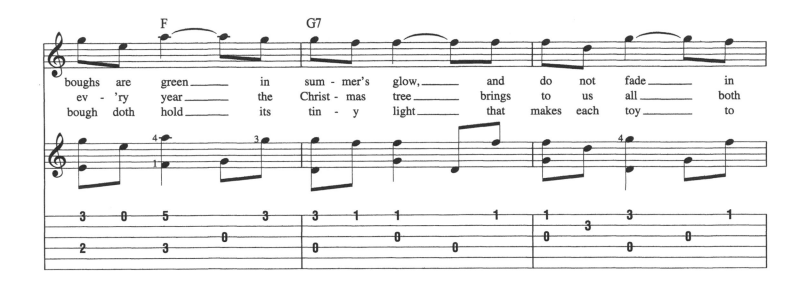

boughs are green in sum-mer's glow, and do not fade in
ev-'ry year the Christ-mas tree brings to us all both
bough doth hold its tin-y light that makes each toy to

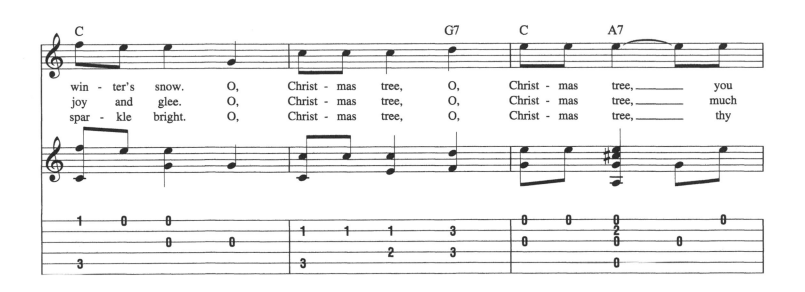

win-ter's snow. O, Christ-mas tree, O, Christ-mas tree, you
joy and glee. O, Christ-mas tree, O, Christ-mas tree, much
spar-kle bright. O, Christ-mas tree, O, Christ-mas tree, thy

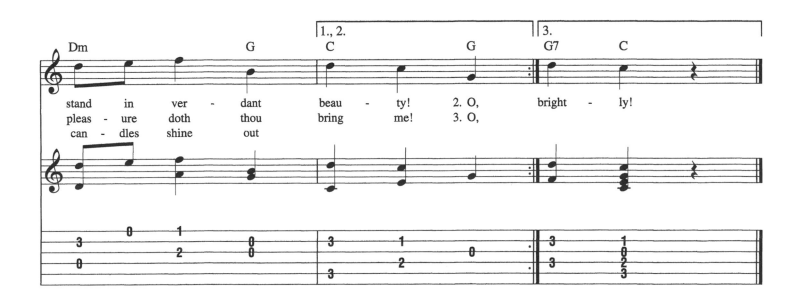

stand in ver-dant beau-ty! 2. O, bright-ly!
pleas-ure doth thou bring me! 3. O,
can-dles shine out

O Come, All Ye Faithful
(Adeste Fideles)

Words and Music by John Francis Wade
Latin Words translated by Frederick Oakeley

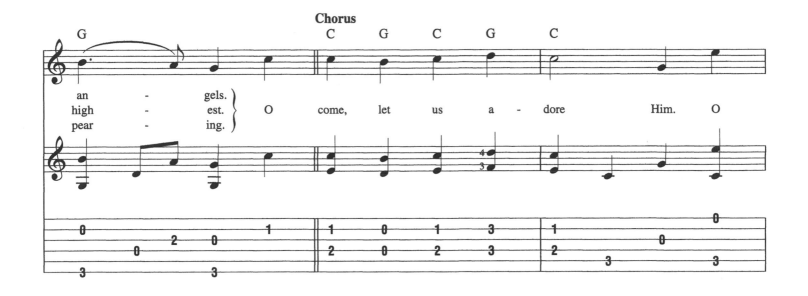

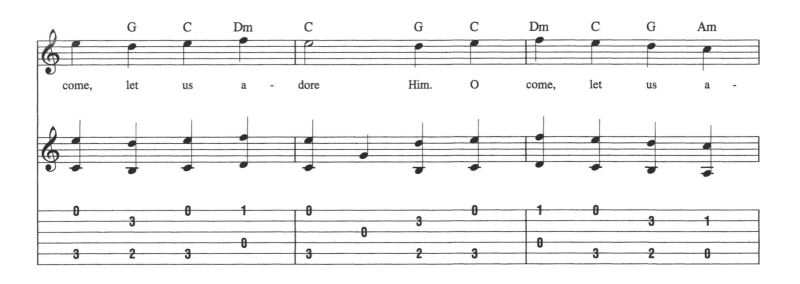

O Little Town of Bethlehem

Words by Phillips Brooks
Music by Lewis H. Redner

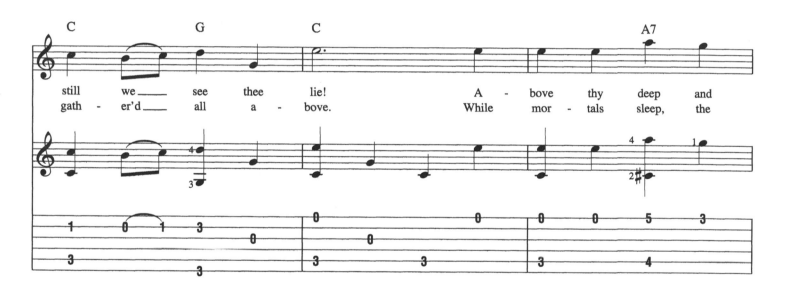

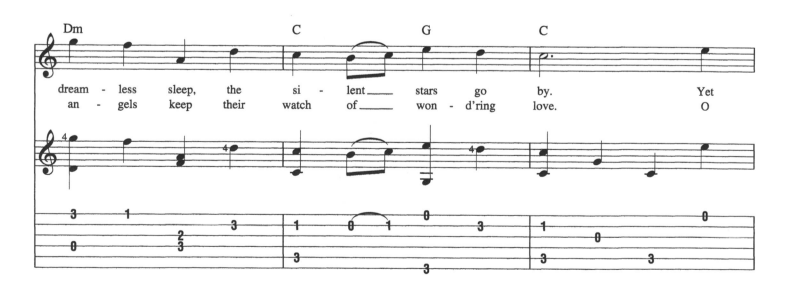

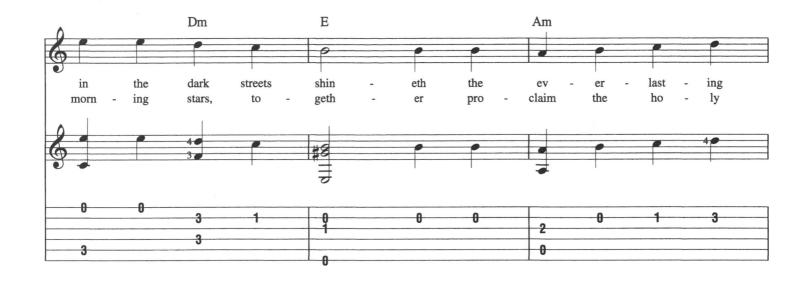

in the dark streets shin - eth the ev - er - last - ing
morn - ing stars, to - geth - er pro - claim the ho - ly

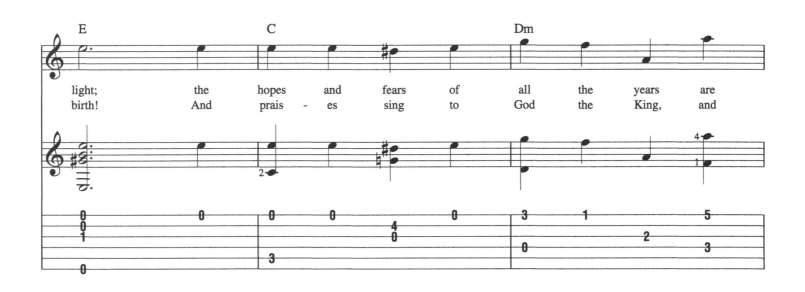

light; the hopes and fears of all the years are
birth! And prais - es sing to God the King, and

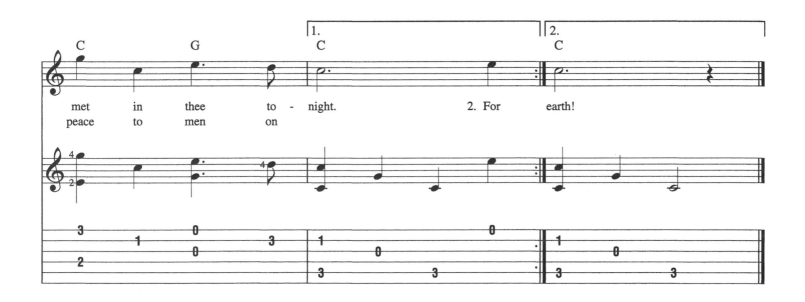

met in thee to - night. 2. For earth!
peace to men on

Silent Night

Words by Joseph Mohr
Translated by John F. Young
Music by Franz X. Gruber

1. Si - lent night, ho - ly night!
2. Si - lent night, ho - ly night!
3. Si - lent night, ho - ly night!

All is calm, all is bright.
Shep - herds quake at the sight.
Son of God, love's pure light.

Round yon vir - gin moth - er and child.
Glo - ries stream from heav - en a - far.
Ra - d'ant beams from Thy ho - ly face

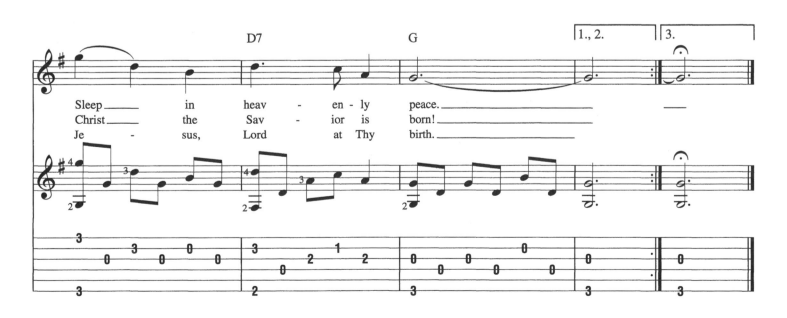

Up on the Housetop

Words and Music by B.R. Handy

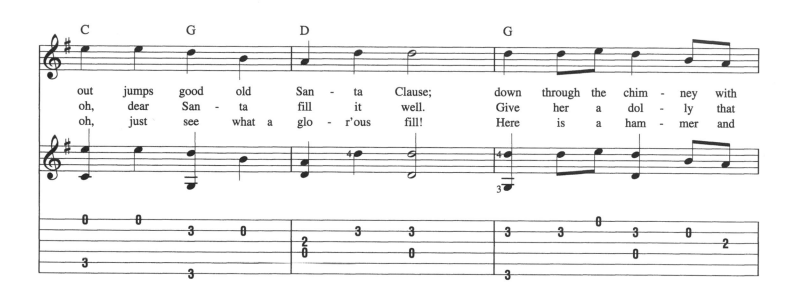

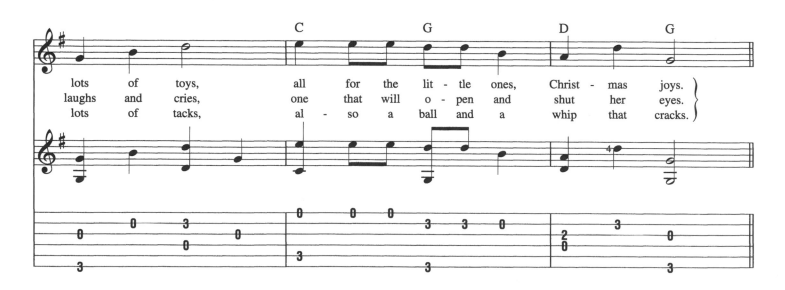

Chorus

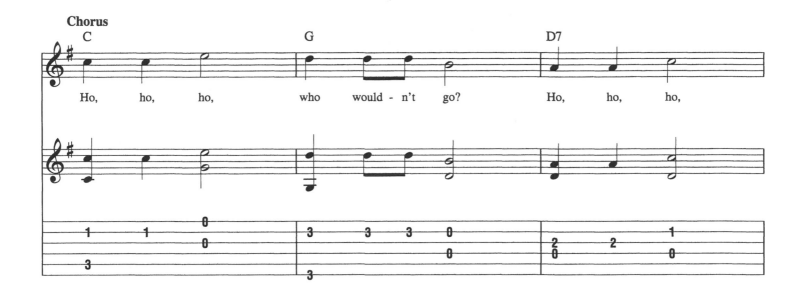

Ho, ho, ho, who would-n't go? Ho, ho, ho,

who would-n't go?____ Up on the house-top, click, click, click.

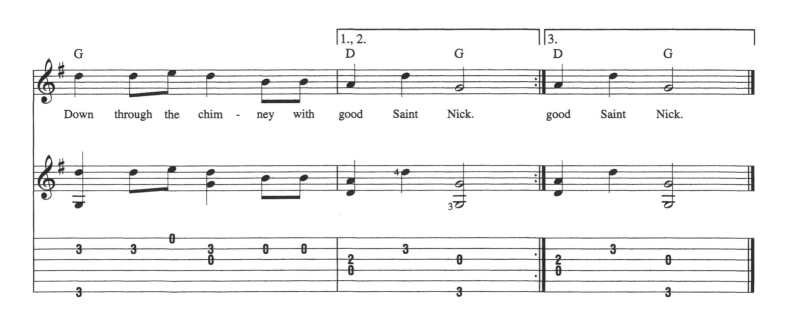

Down through the chim-ney with good Saint Nick. good Saint Nick.

We Three Kings of Orient Are

Words and Music by John H. Hopkins, Jr.

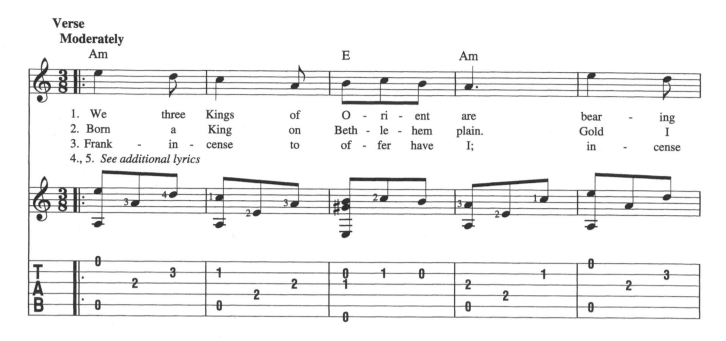

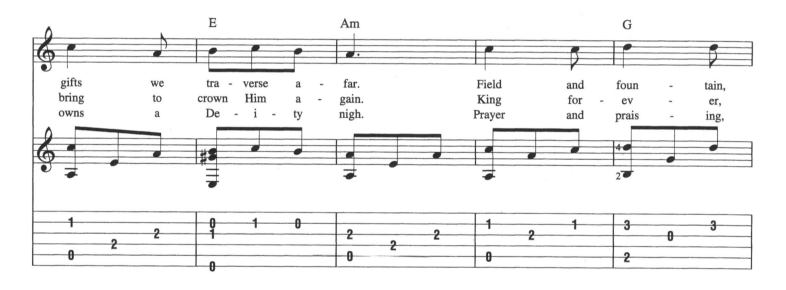

Chorus

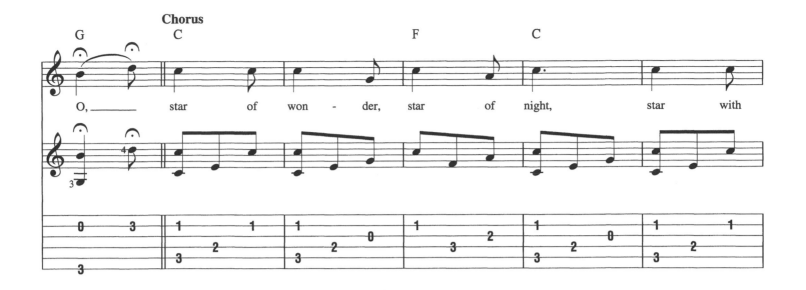

O, _____ star of won - der, star of night, star with

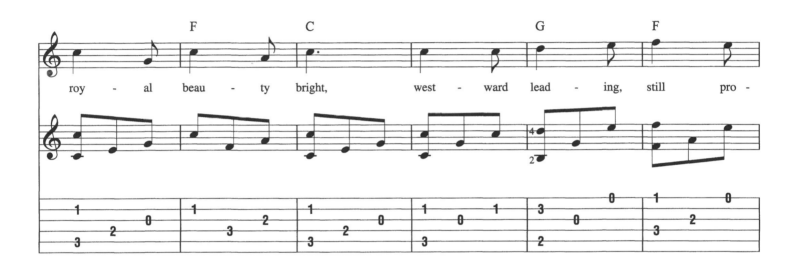

roy - al beau - ty bright, west - ward lead - ing, still pro -

ceed - ing, guide us to thy per - fect light. light.

Additional Lyrics

4. Myrrh is mine: its bitter perfume
Breathes a life of gathering gloom.
Sorrowing, sighing, bleeding, dying;
Sealed in the stone-cold tomb.

5. Glorious now, behold Him arise,
King and God, and Sacrifice!
Heav'n sings alleluia,
Alleluia, the earth replies:

What Child Is This?

Words by William C. Dix
16th Century English Melody

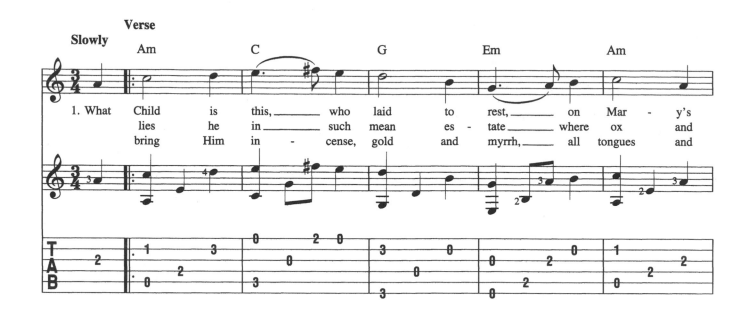

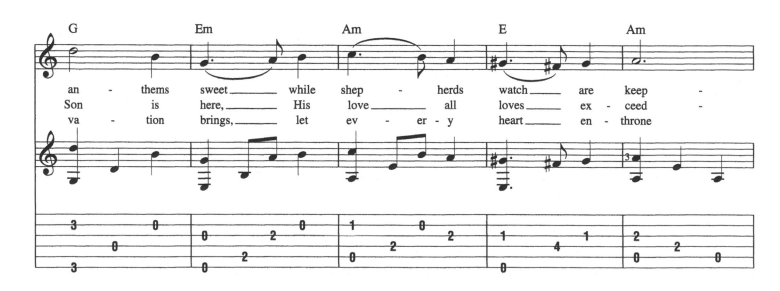

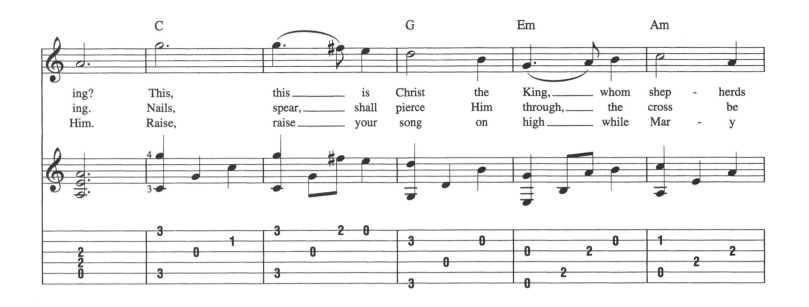

ing?　This,　this＿＿＿ is Christ the King,＿＿＿ whom shep - herds
ing.　Nails,　spear,＿＿＿ shall pierce Him through,＿＿＿ the cross be
Him.　Raise,　raise＿＿＿ your song on high＿＿＿ while Mar - y

guard＿＿＿ and an - gels sing:　Haste,　haste＿＿＿ to bring him
borne＿＿＿ for me and you.　Hail,　hail＿＿＿ the Sav - iour
sings＿＿＿ a lul - la - by.　Joy,　joy＿＿＿ for Christ is

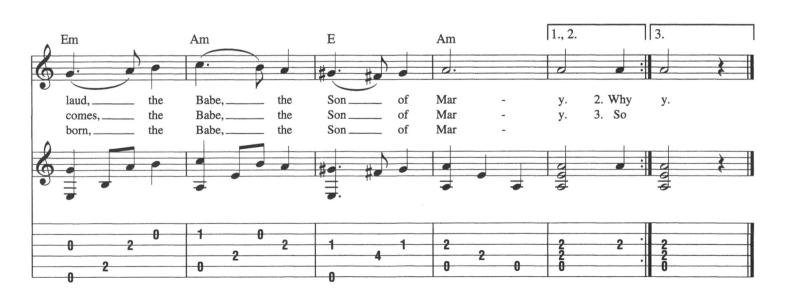

laud,＿＿＿ the Babe,＿＿＿ the Son＿＿＿ of Mar - y. 2. Why y.
comes,＿＿＿ the Babe,＿＿＿ the Son＿＿＿ of Mar - y. 3. So
born,＿＿＿ the Babe,＿＿＿ the Son＿＿＿ of Mar -

We Wish You a Merry Christmas

Traditional English Folksong

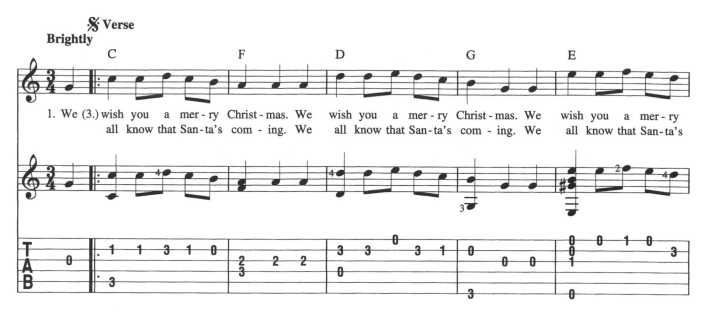

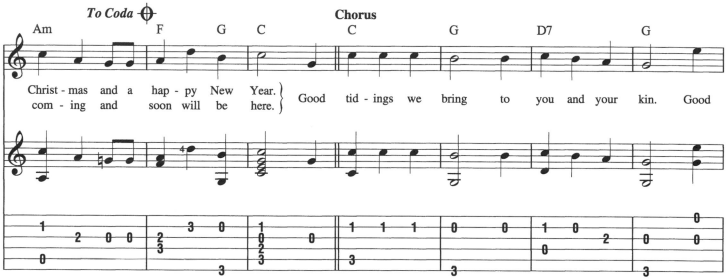

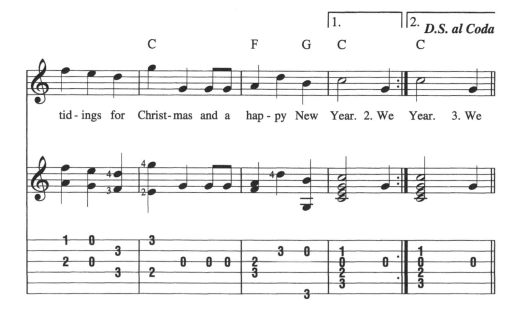